Garbage Trucks
on the Go

by Beth Bence Reinke

BUMBA BOOKS™

LERNER PUBLICATIONS ◆ MINNEAPOLIS

Note to Educators:

Throughout this book, you'll find critical thinking questions. These can be used to engage young readers in thinking critically about the topic and in using the text and photos to do so.

Lerner Publications Company
A division of Lerner Publishing Group, Inc.
241 First Avenue North
Minneapolis, MN 55401 USA

For reading levels and more information, look up this title at www.lernerbooks.com.

Library of Congress Cataloging-in-Publication Data

The Cataloging-in-Publication Data for *Garbage Trucks on the Go* is on file at the Library of Congress.
978-1-5124-8253-9 (lib. bdg.)
978-1-5415-1113-2 (pbk.)
978-1-5124-8257-7 (EB pdf)

Manufactured in the United States of America
1 – CG – 12/31/17

Expand learning beyond the printed book. Download free, complementary educational resources for this book from our website, www.lerneresource.com.

Table of
Contents

Garbage Trucks

Garbage trucks are

big machines.

They pick up trash and take

it away.

Garbage collectors drive garbage trucks. Some collectors put the trash into the truck.

Recycling trucks are a kind

of garbage truck.

They pick up the items we recycle.

What kinds of items can we recycle?

This garbage truck is a

rear loader.

The trash goes in the back.

A packer blade crushes the trash.

It will make room for more.

Why do you think garbage trucks need a packer blade?

packer blade

13

Side loaders have an arm.

The arm grabs the bin.

It lifts and tilts the bin.

It dumps the trash into the truck.

This garbage truck

has forks.

The forks lift the dumpster.

They tip and dump the

trash out.

The garbage truck is full.

It drives to a station.

Recycled items are sorted.

Other trash goes to a landfill.

Where else might trash go?

Garbage trucks help keep our community clean. Does a garbage truck pick up your trash?

Parts of a Garbage Truck

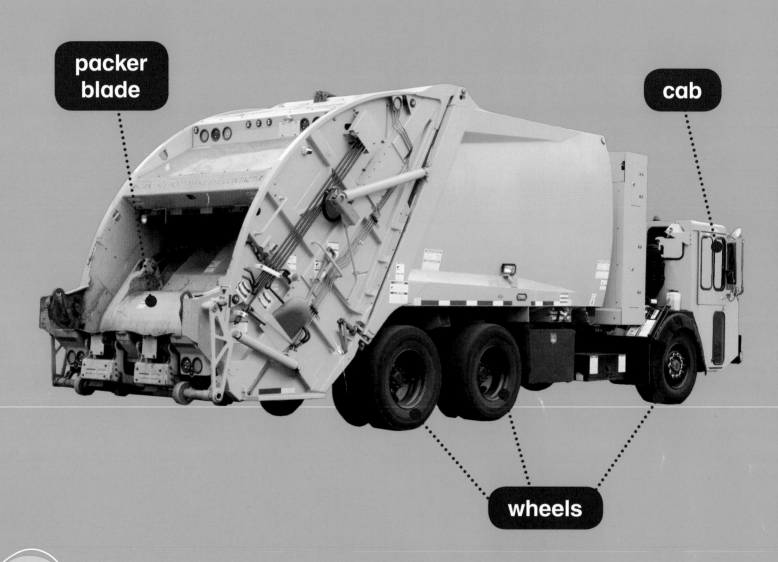

packer blade

cab

wheels

Picture Glossary

forks

two long metal spikes on the front of a garbage truck

landfill

an area where trash is dumped and buried

packer blade

a metal blade that smashes down garbage

recycle

to use old items to make new products

23

Read More

Heos, Bridget. *Follow that Garbage! A Journey to the Landfill.* Mankato, MN: Amicus, 2017.

Kenan, Tessa. *Hooray for Garbage Collectors!* Minneapolis: Lerner Publications, 2018.

Meister, Cari. *Garbage Trucks.* Jump!, 2014.

Index

Photo Credits